MY ENCOUNTER WITH *Angels*

DR. JUANITA WOODSON

Copyright © 2019 by Dr. Juanita Woodson

All rights reserved. This book or any portion thereof may not be reproduced or used in any manner whatsoever without the express written permission of the publisher except for the use of brief quotations in a book review.

Scriptures marked KJV are taken from the KING JAMES VERSION (KJV): KING JAMES VERSION, public domain.

Scriptures marked ESV are taken from the THE HOLY BIBLE, ENGLISH STANDARD VERSION (ESV): Scriptures taken from THE HOLY BIBLE, ENGLISH STANDARD VERSION ® Copyright© 2001 by Crossway, a publishing ministry of Good News Publishers. Used by permission.

Scriptures marked AMP are taken from the AMPLIFIED BIBLE (AMP): Scripture taken from the AMPLIFIED® BIBLE, Copyright © 1954, 1958, 1962, 1964, 1965, 1987 by the Lockman Foundation Used by Permission. (www.Lockman.org)

ISBN - 978-1-7330800-0-2

Printed in the United States of America

First Printing, 2019

Impact Development Foundation Inc.

Impact Book Publishing Co

950 Eagles Landing Pkwy
Suite #722
Stockbridge GA, 30281
www.DrJuanitaWoodson.com
www.impactbookco.com

Table of Contents

* * * * * *

Foreword... 1

Introduction By Dr. Juanita Woodson 5

    Angel of Healing 5

    Angelic Experience at Lenika's House 9

    My Prayer Room 11

    Jewels from Heaven 13

    Personal Angels 15

Contributions...................................... 19

    Melissa Osman................................ 21

    Alicia Isreal Campbell......................... 27

    Sherilyn Bennett.............................. 31

    Bwana Holmes................................ 35

Chapter 1: Encounter of 4 Angels By Christina Knight 41

Encounter # 1: The Angel Who Carried the Cross . . 43

Encounter # 2: The Angels at The Bedside 47

Encounter # 3: Dispatching of Angels 51

Encounter # 4: The Kneeling Ange and The Angels of Help... .55

Chapter 2: Dancing with the Angels By Zernon S. Evans 59

Chapter 3: Aagels & Worship By Annette Birdsong . . 69

Chapter 4: Lifted and Delivered By Lolitia Newman . 81

Chapter 5: Invoking Angelic Release By Jennifer Washington .... .89

Chapter 6: The Delta By Antonico Thomas 99

Dr. Juanita Woodson 105

Foreword

* * * * * *

It is Indeed an honor and privilege to write this book foreword for this beautiful woman of God. Apostle Juanita and I connected years ago when I reached out to her for ministry assistance! She immediately responded to help answer my questions and from there a relationship was birthed.

That was years ago and since then I've learned so much from her but most importantly, I've discovered that she is truly someone you need in your circle. A true daughter of The King whom He uses to set the captives free. She has been chosen because of her passion for healing and deliverance to those in bondage, crossing boundaries to see this accomplished. When going into battle, it is an honor to have her on your side.

Armed and very knowledgeable of spiritual warfare Apostle Juanita is definitely equipped to deliver information on this subject matter!

"My Encounter with Angels" will shed light of

the supernatural existence of God's holy warriors offering hope to believers that we are not here alone. During times of great pain, suffering and battles, angels are ever so present helping us alone the way.

With each angelic account shared in this book, it offers hope to the reader that you are not alone even when it feels as though you are, God's angels are there ready to win battles for you on the battle ground.

From Genesis to Revelation there are many accounts of angels that include great details about them in the Word of God. If angels were not significant or important God would not have created them, therefore their very existence is necessary.

It was very encouraging to see another book written on this powerful subject matter because I personally believe the body of Christ has studied about demons and deliverance for far so long, allowing the teaching of angels to become minimized. This is not to minimize revelation that comes from being knowledgeable in the area of deliverance as it too is supernatural, however we must be aware of the assistance of these holy and divine creatures and we must be open to their presence and existence because of the great mission they are assigned, as they help believers with the will of God being accomplished in the earth.

Allow your faith to be increased as you press in to believe the impossible while gaining knowledge and revelation. If God allowed these individuals to experience angelic encounters, also believe that He can do the same for you!

It is my prayer this book will offer much hope, inspiration, and encouragement to the reader. Your faith and hunger for "Angelic Encounters" and supernatural experiences will increase!

Prophetess
Lenika Scott
Author of Angelic Allies

MY ENCOUNTER WITH ANGELS

Introduction
By Dr. Juanita Woodson

ANGEL OF HEALING
* * * * *

I had just given birth to a beautiful baby girl who for once, looked just like me. The doctor had just come into my labor and delivery room making his usual rounds to all the new mothers who had recently given birth. As I anxiously awaited my discharge papers to take me and my new baby girl home, a nurse suggested that we wait a little longer. No problem I thought, maybe they have some more paper work and we would surely be home soon. After a few minutes a nurse came and and said we need to put the baby on a little oxygen because she needs a little more air. The brought a small tube with two little prongs that would rest right under her tiny nose and blow up air. After about an hour they noticed she needed even more air and they put the little cup over her nose and mouth.

Each hour they came and checked on her and turned the oxygen machine up higher and higher. Finally, the machine could not go any higher and the doctor came in to speak with me. They advised that my daughter was not breathing on her own and that they would have to put tubes down her throat so that she would have oxygen go straight to her lungs. I was terrified! I was not allowed to be a part of the procedure, but they put her into a comma so that she would not fight the process. I wept and wept sorely as I didn't understand why my baby had to endure such invasive procedures. She was in ICU full of about 6 or 7 tubes for different purposes.

I was in shock. It was 3 full days and I was forced to go home because there was no more room for me. My

INTRODUCTION

father came to visit me and told me that God wanted me to repent and to surrender and that I should go on a fast. I repented before God for running from my ministry and I submitted my will to Him that day. I went on a 3 day no food and no water fast. I wanted God to turn my baby's life around and save her! Three more days went by with no change. I could not breast feed her nor bottle feed her.

She was being fed through tubes in her belly. I went home that night believing that some way somehow a miracle had to happen, I was accepting nothing less. The next morning on the 7th day I went to the hospital to spend time with her and I was greeted by the doctor before going in. I was extremely optimistic but very concerned about what she would tell me.

She said "I don't know what happened, but your baby is breathing on her own. Last night she took all her tubes out and laid it beside her, we have no idea how that happened. She's too little to do that and she was in a comma. She's breathing like a normal healthy baby." God spoke to me and said an angel came and removed the tubes because she was healed. I cried and cried! I rejoiced and rejoiced! How do I know angels are real? Because one of them came and healed my baby under the instructions and direction of God.

MY ENCOUNTER WITH ANGELS

INTRODUCTION

ANGELIC EXPERIENCE AT LENIKA'S HOUSE

* * * * *

A good friend of mine named Lenika Scott has a unique ability to sense the presence of angels. She would find angel feathers around the house and eventually began to find heavenly jewels. Her prayer room was a room that angels would hang out and carry out the prayers that were prayed. I came to visit her once at her home and was offered the unique opportunity to sleep in her prayer room.

During my time in the prayer room God visited me and began to reveal many things to me about my life and what was to happen. I asked God to allow me to receive an angel feather before I left. It got down to the last day and still no feather. As I packed up my things and talked with Lenika and a good friend Danita Hayes, I began to realize that my desire for a feather would not happen.

Just as we were about to leave I felt a poke in my back. At first I ignored it because I thought I had something in my pocket. The poke continued until I took notice and reached behind me. When I grabbed the thing that poked me, I realized that it was a beautiful large feather! I could not believe it! I told Lenika and Danita that they would never believe what I had received, and I pulled out this gorgeous feather! Everyone was in utter awe and Danita began to instantly cry. We couldn't believe that at the last minute, God granted my request to receive a feather! Since that time, I have also made a prayer room in my house and have had angelic visitations as well as jewels manifestation.

INTRODUCTION

MY PRAYER ROOM

* * * * *

One day I decided to have an entire prayer room in my house. I was currently using my closet and I wanted to dedicate more space to God for prayer. My nanny and I designed the room and purchased the most beautiful pieces to go inside. After decorating and setting up the room I prayed a prayer to the Lord that He and His angels would be in the room and abide with us. I asked God to answer prayers and deliver His people when I came to pray in the room.

After a long day out running errands, I decided to visit my prayer room and spend some time with God. Upon opening the door, something stood up from my ottoman. I literally saw the indention in the seat and the pressure release upon something standing up. I was so livid! I started rebuking the devil and demons and all sorts of evil things out my prayer room. I did that for almost two hours, cleansing the atmosphere and house. I sent things to the dry place and I commanded them never to return! I could not believe the devil came in my prayer room! I felt great peace fall upon me and I went to bed.

The next morning as I was eating breakfast, the Lord spoke to me. It was a still soft voice. He said, "You know, you told me you wanted Me and the angels to be in the prayer room." I immediately began to repent and ask God for forgiveness! I was so used to battling demons that I didn't know when it was angelic attendance. Wow, I had to change my view point to the fact that every presence is not demonic. We as believers can spend way too much time fighting the devil instead of employing our God given help.

INTRODUCTION

JEWELS FROM HEAVEN

* * * * *

I continued to have close encounters with angels often. One day I went to a meeting and I was sitting in the waiting room. I kept seeing a sparkle out of the side of my eye and it appeared to be intentionally shiny my way. The more I ignored it, the brighter it became. I got up from the sofa and went over to the sparkle and picked up what appeared to be a jewel. It was a loose stone that appeared to have fallen out of someones, ring but whose? Just then I realized I had prayed and asked God to give me jewels from heaven like others had experienced. As I walked back to the sofa I saw two more sparkles and they were identical to the first. They were gold in hue and very well defined as jewels. I was ecstatic! I could not believe that God allowed me to receive not just one stone but three! Three represents the totality of God and a cord that cannot be easily broken! God is so faithful!

INTRODUCTION

PERSONAL ANGELS

* * * * *

Soon after finding the stones, I hit a bout of extreme depression. Depression on a level so strong that I thought I would actually lose my mind. Literally out of nowhere and for no reason I could think of, I was slipping into something bigger than me! I called people to pray but no one was available. I rebuked and bind all the demons I could think of. I spoke in all my warfare tongues with no relief. Extreme desperation set in and I went into the middle of my living room and shouted, "Father make the devil leave me alone, I can't do it myself!" Immediately the pressure and depression left.

I began to weep and worship God with all my might, I tried to fall on my face, but something held me up. My arms lifted up supernaturally and God said, "Let me fill you up." I felt warmth cover me inside and out and I stood with the strength of God. Just then I saw two beings behind me. One on the left and one on the right. Suddenly I was released from being held and I fell on the sofa and wept. One of the beings came over to my left side and kneeled with me, it almost seemed to want to comfort me. God said, "This is your angel who will be with you and help you throughout your life."

He revealed the angel's function, but I'd rather not share it. I felt a presence on my right side moving about in the air. As I looked to my right, I saw three small angels floating in the air with wings. God said to me, "These are angels of miracles, signs, and wonders. They will follow you the rest of your life." I cried and cried; I could not believe what I was seeing and experiencing!

After the Spirit lifted some, I got up and went to the bathroom. On the floor I found a gold tone pearl. I tried to find an outfit or necklace that it belonged to, but I could not find anything it went to. I realized I had received a pearl from heaven. I was out of it at this point. Immediately my phone rang, and it was

INTRODUCTION

someone who needed prayer. She was going through terrible defeat and depression. I was so full at that point that I went all in on that prayer! I asked God to do what He did for me earlier and I asked him as "Father" to go get the devil off this person and make him leave her alone! The prayer was awesome, and I knew it was successful.

When I finished praying, the lady said something amazing to me, she said, "When you told God to go get the devil off me, I saw a very large angel with wings of fire and a huge sword standing behind you!" She said that this angel was with me to help God's people. I began to worship again. I told her how I almost lost my mind earlier that day, but God sent this angel to help me. I told her how I called on God like He was my natural Father not a distant being, and He rushed to my aid!

I want everyone reading this book to grab on to faith understanding that we have a God that loves us and wants to help us. There is supernatural help readily available to assist us in life. We need to become more aware of all the tools God has provided. We are not in this walk of life by ourselves. We have God, each other, and angels. Allow the stories of this book to enlighten your sense of the supernatural existence and to believe that anything is possible with God's help!

With love,
Dr. Juanita Woodson
www.DrJuanitaWoodson.com

Contributions

MY ENCOUNTER WITH ANGELS

MELISSA OSMAN

* * * * *

It was a warm, rainy morning in early June when my husband and I made a second attempt to legalize our marriage in the small town of Camden Georgia. After being turned away the day before they informed us that they were only open certain days of the week to obtain a marriage license. If we wanted to obtain one that day then we needed to go to another County. After much discussion my Husband, Mother in law, Pastor and I decided to go to the small City of Folkston Georgia which is in Charlton County Georgia to obtain the license. Before we were able to get into our truck, we were approached by a guy who asked if we had any jumper cables to assist him in getting his vehicle started which was further up in a parking space near the exit of the Court House.

As we had agreed, before we exited the parking lot we stopped to help the guy to get his vehicle started. The relief on his face was visible. He told us he asked several people, but we were the only ones who took the time to help him. He tried to give us money for helping him but of course we refused to take it. We asked that he go ahead of us and we would go out behind after him. As soon as he turned to leave he disappeared. My husband and I were so astonished the only thing we could figure out was he was an Angel.

We soon reached our destination to obtain our legal marriage license, filled out the paper work and headed out the door. The court house wanted My Pastor to do a ceremony with us at the court house that day at that moment. Due to the conflict with the Camden Court House the day prior the ceremony had already taken place the night before. So, we drove down the road to a nearby Burger King to finish signing the documents. I had to use the bathroom, so I went into the Burger King to find out that the Women's Restroom was closed due to being cleaned. I came back out and asked my husband to please drive me next door so I could go. He did take me next door which was a community pharmacy.

My Mother in Law and I went inside while my husband waited outside for my Pastor to show back up with all the proper documentation concerning our Marriage License. While in the restroom I heard some commotion going on out the door. My husband called me on my cellphone asking if I see any issues with showing his ID to assist a guy to be able to purchase his medicine. I talked to the pharmacist to clear any and all liability from my husband and told him go ahead. The guy was buying a prescription that required an ID and he did not have an ID.

My husband says he asked many people that turned him away, but he decided to try one more time. My husband said he had to help. Leaving the pharmacy as my husband explained what this guy looked like I said, "Wait a minute, that's the guy I didn't know where he came from when we drove in." We again discussed it and decided he must have been another Angel.

We went back to Burger King to buy something to eat because we were running late to pick up our puppy Shiloh for the first time. After we ordered our food my husband accidently drove over the curb. I asked him to please park the truck and eat so he could gain some strength. He agreed and we parked our truck away from Burger King facing the Pharmacy. As we were sitting there finishing our prayer and starting to eat our meal I noticed a Lady who appeared to be disabled chasing a young boy running around the back of the pharmacy. When the little boy ran out from behind the building I noticed he clearly had Down syndrome and Autism which I have had past experience as well as training to assist special needs children.

    I looked at my husband and told him, "We have to get this boy before he runs into the street". My husband who has scoliosis and has difficulties even walking himself jumped out of the truck, running as fast as we had ever seen him be able to move, he tackled the little boy to the ground inches before he got to the road. I ran in close behind my husband sitting down to cradle the little boy. His grandmother soon came and sat down beside us out of breath and relieved we had caught him in time. She explained to me the hardships that her, her son and grandson were going through.

She began to cry and I held her with my other arm while continuing to calm the little boy down. My husband walked back to our truck and pulled up beside us closer. With permission my husband allowed the little boy to watch a cartoon on his phone and eat some fries while the little boy's grandma pulled her station wagon to get her grandson back in her car. After asking if she needed anything else and helping her get the little boy back into her car she thanked us saying, "All these people around here and y'all are the only ones who took up the time to help." Just as fast as we turned around to get in our truck her little car disappeared. The only entrance or exit was too far to move that fast onto that busy street. My mother in law was in the truck crying and you could feel the spirit of God all in our truck. I believe the angels were sent to see if we were going to slow down to take the time to serve him.

MY ENCOUNTER WITH ANGELS

ALICIA ISREAL CAMPBELL

* * * * *

When I lived in California, I was walking home through an apartment complex. I was singing praises unto the Lord. As I was walking i came across a man standing in his doorway. He spoke softly to me and ask me to come in he wanted to show me something. I said Sir I don't know you and he replied back and said yes you do. You accepted me into your life. I said sir the only person I accepted in my life was my husband and Jesus. That is true and I am him. The door opens wider and all I seen was white carpet and red trimming.

Everything in the house was white clean trimmed in read and beautiful. I started crying because of the overwhelming peace. I explained that I couldn't walk in the house because of my shoes. I took them off and walked in and he began to tell me of my life and the things I would endure. He said embrace yourself because your road would not be easy. I began to cry again. I explained I have to tell my husband about you, and He said no one could know about our visit nor his place. But i left and told my husband because I was so excited. When i brought my husband and a few friends back with me the places were boarded up.

The Landlord came by and ask what we were looking for and I said the man who lives here. The Landlord said sweetie this apartment is vacant, and I said sir I just was her speaking to the man in this very apartment #3. He said sweetie this apartment has been vacant for 7 years. It was a fire, and someone died in this apartment and I never fixed repaired it to rent it out. I again said sir there is a man who lives here, and his apartment is all white trimmed in red on the inside. I said open it up and you will see. The Landlord open the door and the house was horrible and it stunk really bad. I cried because I knew I wasn't crazy. He said I'm sorry, but I told you no one lives here. I even describe the man. He was the man who died in the house. He came and appear to me in as an angel to tell me about my life. I gave my life over to Christ completely and I never spoke of this again because everyone thought I was crazy. But I remember he said no one was supposed to know about our conversation and know of this place. He told me my life and what I would say would upset people because of the call on my life.

Apostle/Prophetess
Alicia Isreal Campbell

MY ENCOUNTER WITH ANGELS

SHERILYN BENNETT

* * * * *

It still seems strange that I am writing this about my encounter because I in many ways still can't believe it happened. I wonder why me. I feel so chosen and special because of it and I do feel my life has changed spiritually since then. It is interesting because the place where I had the encounter I no longer live. I struggled with finding peace there and my apartment manager eventually moved me to another unit.

I remember it like it just happened. The experience is totally and will forever be etched in my heart and mind. My mother and sons were visiting me in Charlotte for the Christmas holiday. It was a normal day and night. I actually slept next to my mother that night and my sons were sprawled out in the living room. I was got up around 6 AM on Christmas morning and to go to the restroom. As I exited my room something to the left of me caught my attention. I remember just glancing over and at the same time wondered why a man would be in my living room. The first thing I noticed was that he seemed huge and too big to in my home but there he sat. He was sitting there with his elbow on his knee. He just seemed so huge. He was larger than life, magnificent.

Amazingly I was curious but not afraid. I moved in closer to look a little more intently and I remember thinking he was dark but in actuality he was transparent, and the room was dark. As I looked closer, I noticed feathers or wings laying to his side. He was not a solid figure he was transparent as stated. I could only see the outline of his body. He was not intimidating, and peace surrounded him. He was not disturbed by my inspection of him, but I was in awe. He looked like he was just keeping watch. He certainly didn't look like this was his first rodeo. He was watching. He never moved and neither did my sons.

I was quite startled when I realized what I was seeing. I continued to try and convince myself that wasn't what it was. I remember shaking my head saying under my voice, "No way, that can't be right." As I begin to back away my heart was racing, and I didn't feel like I was in the earthly realm. I was somewhere else. The air was different, and my body acted differently.

I remember turning away and snagging my pajama bottoms on the bathroom door still in total disbelief. Before entering the bathroom, I decided to turn around and confirm what I had seen. When I turned around, he was gone. I could hardly breathe. Why would God show me an angel? That Christmas morning, I had been given the most amazing gift. I was able to see the spirit realm like never before. I went on into the bathroom and tried to calm myself down. I remember saying, God you are so real, everything is going to be ok. God whispered, "Gabriel" I quickly got my bible to remind myself about the angel Gabriel. He had come with a message. What was it you wanted me to know God?

Lastly, I know for a fact that I was changed that day and in the words of my best friend Shonda, I had received the best Christmas gift ever. I have not shared this story with anyone other than a few friends and my aunt before now. I didn't want people to think I had lost my mind; however, I am glad I overcame the fear of telling it. I pray this encounter confirms and blesses someone's life. It sure has changed mine.

Prophetess,
Sherilyn Bennett

BWANA HOLMES

* * * * *

It was approximately 13 years ago when I had my first known angelic encounter. I was at least 4 months pregnant and terribly sick with a disease called Hyperemesis gravidarum (HG). No one told me that a woman could be pregnant and sick as I was. I'd been seeing one doctor who didn't know what to do with me, so he suggested that I terminate the pregnancy. I remember agreeing with him on terminating the pregnancy and then my sister, who I ended up having to live with at the time, went and met with the doctor and that was the end of my visits with him. LOL!

Shortly after the visits with him, I would return to my room upstairs feeling like, God must have been punishing me for getting pregnant out of wedlock. I was an active Worship Leader in my church at the time and was coming into a prophetic awareness of my calling. So, it wasn't like I wasn't saved and didn't know God. I knew Him well and He knew me. I, like any single lady desiring marriage, had become lonely and vulnerable which caused me to land in the state that I was in.

My daily routine consisted of me waking up, being super sensitive to every smell there was including mild powder scents, a nurse coming to our home, changing my pic line, administering meds, and keeping me hydrated, as some days I could barely keep water down! I was mentally and emotionally tired. Lonely, and dreaded carrying my baby to term. I literally wanted to just get rid of the baby and move on with my single life. There were countless times I considered taking a trip to the nearest Abortion Clinic because some would let you term the pregnancy even up to 5 months.

One morning after a routine check in with my sister, she left for work and I decided to just pray and cry out to the Lord! I hadn't prayed during this time because I was too sick and felt so condemned! Even after my then Pastor gracefully restored me before the church. I fell to my knees crying and pleading, "Lord PLEASE come see about ME" I am dying! I am sorry and I repent for getting pregnant out of wedlock! PLEASE don't let me continue to suffer"! These were my exact words. I cried out and then a presence of peace filled my room the entire day. When my sister and my baby's father would check on me, I was at peace. When night came, I fell asleep peacefully and TWO angels came into the room. One would sit in one corner of the room and the other on the opposite side.

The Angels were male and female, dressed in navy blue scrubs. I remember telling them, you may leave me, I'm okay, I said it over and over and they NEVER left! I went to sleep and when I woke up, they were gone. I went and grabbed the phone book (remember those) and opened it to the first set of yellow pages that literally landed on an OBGYN Specialist. I called the office and briefly explained my situation and they asked if I could come in that day.

Although my quality of life wouldn't allow me to drive, I somehow mustered up the strength to go anyway. When I got there, the doctor that I saw on the yellow page ad was there, standing tall and warm. He examined me and said, "I'll have to put you where you don't want to go, BACK to the HOSPITAL". I thought, Lord, NO, but of course I went on. Once I got checked into my room, the same presence that visited me in my bedroom the night before the Angels came in, came into my hospital room. I began to weep uncontrollably as a female Nurse came through my doors with NAVY BLUE SCRUBS on! She asked, "Are you okay sweetheart"?

We are going to take good care of you. I could hardly respond as she continued to prep me to be seen by the doctor. Once she was done, she said, "You won't see me again, I'm gone on vacation" but before she left the room, in came the doctor from the visit with NAVY BLUE SCRUBS on!

I nearly fainted and they both said, "Hey you're going to be okay, don't cry".. I said you wouldn't understand it, but I know for sure I'm going to be okay as I continued to weep! I won't say that I never believed in Angels, but I never thought, as a believer we could encounter such an expression of Abba's love. Because of the love of our Father and the Angels that were assigned to my life to carry him, my firstborn, Zebediah (a gift from Abba) lives as an ever-present witness that Angelic encounters are real, and they are of the Lord.

Prophetess
Bwana Holmes

MY ENCOUNTER WITH ANGELS

Chapter 1
Encounter of 4 Angels
By Christina Knight

MY ENCOUNTER WITH ANGELS

Encounter # 1

THE ANGEL WHO CARRIED THE CROSS

* * * * *

I remember like yesterday traveling on the highway one hot summer day with my mom. We had seen something that at first, didn't seem to mean much, but was definitely out of the ordinary. We lived in a suburban area and this highway would lead you to the town where we lived called Tarboro. The opposite side would take you away from Tarboro. We traveled this highway a lot and Tarboro was very small. We would travel this highway to get to a nearby city called Rocky Mount which was about15 minutes up the road. Rocky Mount had a lot more restaurants and shopping areas than our city.

One day we were on our usual trip to Rocky Mount when we noticed a man in the heat of the summer dragging what we knew appears to be a huge cross. Please keep in mind this cross was as big as the cross we see in the movies depicting how Jesus carried it. Nothing seemed to distract him. We got off on the exit and the road took us down, around, and back up which allowed us to view the man from the other side of the highway. My mother and I looped the exit one more time to get a second look at this man because it was so bazar and exciting at the same time.

I happen to look over in the lane beside us and I saw my aunt traveling on the opposite side and said, "look ma there is Aunt Reta!"" Call her and tell her to look at the man with the cross." Immediately my mom called her. My mom was telling her about the man we saw. She told us she did not see him. My mom said Reta we just passed him he is there. So she turned off the exit, and went down to come back up to look for the man and she said "no there is no man there. I'm telling you there is no man." We were so confused, we knew the man was there, there was no way she could have passed him and not saw him and no way he could have gotten to an exit that fast dragging a heavy cross.

At that point in my adult Christian life, I was very young in the things of God. Today, when things happen out of the ordinary, now I tend to pay more attention and try to find a meaning, or a message from the messenger, God! For example, if this was to happen today, I would say, "ok God what are you saying? What does this mean?" I would reference some scriptures and ask Holy Spirit to guide me. So, I found these scriptures from the Bible.

"If anyone would come after me, he must deny himself and take up his cross daily and follow me" (Luke 9:23).

"Anyone who does not carry his cross and follow me cannot be my disciple" (Luke 14:27).

"Not My will, but Yours, be done." Luke 22:42.

Well my question now is What does this mean to you? I can surely tell you what it means to me. I feel it means to put to death your old self. No matter the cost. To totally die to self, and be willing to sacrifice your own desires, and totally commit to be a daily vessel of Christ.

Being a Christian is a daily ongoing sacrifice. In being a Christian, along the way we may lose friends, and activities we normally would enjoy, jobs, and etc. The key is no matter what, continue to take up your cross to reap the final reward. Spending eternity with the father! Which is a far greater reward than anything on earth. Back then the cross was used as a form of punishment for wrong doers and used to make them carry it til death.

I am confident the angel we saw carrying the cross was symbolizing this very message. What I observed was him carrying the heavy cross In the heat of the day. It appeared as a struggle but as the cars passed by him, he continued to carry the cross. Nothing seemed to affect him. His focus was on carrying his cross and reaching his final destination! Amen! Thank you God, for revelation and your angel who represented your message! You see I feel the angel was meant for only us to see so we would realize that this was an angel, and angel who had a special message just for us!

Encounter # 2
THE ANGELS AT THE BEDSIDE
* * * * *

I remember my grandmother so clear as though she never left us. My grandmom, as we affectionately called her, was the type of southern grandmom who would break out in and old hymn about Jesus anytime. Especially when she was in her home, where I often spent time as a child. She was the grandmom who said, "girl don't question God, and say your prayers before you go to bed." She also was the grandmom who would see fault but seemed to forgive no matter what. I remember being in my first marriage and my husband brutally beat me and hid me for a night. I returned home with two black eyes, prints in my face from being kicked, and a limp that ended up causing physical therapy. When my grandmom saw me she said, "Lord what's wrong with that boy, Lord help him!" That's what she cried out to God. Why did she pray for him? Wasn't I the victim? I remember one of my aunts saying nothing's wrong with him mama he's just nasty. Please!

In looking back on this, my grandmom taught me the true meaning of a very powerful tool! Forgiveness. At this age forgiveness never came by easy with me. I never really knew why it was necessary but that I was told a Christian I had to do it. Small things like this were always happening when around grandma that gave us all examples of how we were to behave as Christians.

However, one example clearly sticks out in my memory. It took place in my late twenties. It was the passing of my grandmom. I remember being in her hospital room, like yesterday. She looked at me and said something that changed my life for the worst. She said, "Christina I'm leaving this world." I said, "grandma don't say that, no you're not." She said, "yes I am. The angels are all around my bed. They are waiting on me." So I'm standing there like what in the world?! No one was in the room at this time but me and her. She also shared with us that a lot of people days were numbered and that a large number of them will leave at the same time. This was so weird to me. Whose days were numbered why did they all have to leave?

After this, my grandmom begin to quote scriptures over and over again. She quoted scriptures until she took her last breath. On September the 11th 2001 we buried my grandmom. On the day of her funeral something tragic happened in America. We realized the massive death toll she was talking about, the event that took place on 9/11! Numerous people did die, and they died all at one time. At this point, I remember thinking to myself, the angels must have really been there too and had to have share with her about 9/11, how else would she have known?

Encounter 3
DISPATCHING OF ANGELS
* * * * *

I remember after my mom passed away; life began to be very hard. A lot of things happened that challenged my faith and caused me to feel alone. My mom was my best friend and losing her made me feel even more alone. When this happened, I turned to God. This was something I had learned from my mom. I would begin flipping through her old bible and started reading scriptures she had jotted down. I would look them up and try to gather understanding of them.

I watched a lot of Facebook videos with pretty much anything concerning God. In doing so I became more and more curious about God. I found myself waking up early to jump on prayer calls, staying up late at night to hear ministers do lives on Facebook, being excited about going to church and barely being able to wait till the next Sunday. I always wanted to be in service, or on Facebook watching just to hear Sundays message! I began to read books about Christianity. In doing this my spirit truly awakened. I found that it was much more to Christianity than I had known! This was exciting to me! I began to read books about the spirit realm, angels, signs and etc. I read on how to dispatch angels! What! I can do that??! During this difficult time of my life, I learned of many of these spiritual things and I would use them. I would always pray and dispatch angels to my Business. When I did this, I would find feathers all over my office just at random. It was continuously! I remember saying to a relative, "I wonder are the angels here?" I asked because the staff was praying together. She said to me, "you said you dispatched them, right?"

I said, "yeah but," then she said, "well ok then, they're there because you sent them there." I remember saying to myself, why can't I find feathers inside my home? Then I heard clearly because you have not dispatched them there! How awesome is Holy Spirit! He leads and guides us from within. So yes, I dispatched them to my home the very next day, I found my first feather in my kitchen, and later I found two on my leg as I was writing this book! I remember reading how as Christians we walk in authority. We as Christians can also speak in authority! That signs follow those that believe. The feathers were signs that the angels were there. I continuously found them because I believed. Lets take a look at these scriptures.

Mark 16:17-18 - And these signs shall follow them that believe; In my name shall they cast out devils; they shall speak with new tongues;

Luke 10:19 - Behold, I give unto you power to tread on serpents and scorpions, and over all the power of the enemy: and nothing shall by any means hurt you.

1 John 5:4-5 - For whatsoever is born of God overcometh the world: and this is the victory that overcometh the world, [even] our faith.

How great is our God! He has given his children the power to overcome the world! Walking by faith and knowing who you are in Christ is very powerful and should be learned by all Christians to exercise in their everyday walk with God.

MY ENCOUNTER WITH ANGELS

Encounter # 4
THE KNEELING ANGEL AND THE ANGELS OF HELP

* * * * *

I went to sleep one night and had a lot on my mind. I was struggling in my personal and business life. However, I remember thinking to myself and telling God many times. I said," God, you said in your word that You would not put more on me than I could bear, well I can't bear anymore." In my prayers I asked for help. I went to bed and something really strange happened. I was standing outside my own body where I experienced seeing myself sleep. A man was kneeling at my bedside and was praying for me. I could hear prayer languages in tongues began to join in with him and pray, I could not see them, but I continued to see him. When I got up the next day, I felt a burden was lifted and peace was restored. I no longer felt troubled about my struggles. I know in my heart the kneeling angel and the other angels whom helped him were sent on assignment to be my comfort and my help! Yes God loves his children and never leaves them! If I could not bear my struggles they would not have been there. Gods plan is perfect with his timing, reason, and purpose for all he does and reveals. Your test is sometimes your testimony! When I came across this scripture; I received confirmation within myself that the angels did indeed come because I cied out to God for help.

Luke 22:42-43 New International Version (NIV)

42 "Father, if you are willing, take this cup from me; yet not my will, but yours be done." **43** An angel from heaven appeared to him and strengthened him. So this is the reason I felt the way I did when I woke up! God knew I needed strength and it was granted! God is so amazing all we have to do is trust him! Learning to trust God has become easy as I grow in my Christian life.

Psalm 28:7 ESV

The Lord is my strength and my shield; in him my heart trusts, and I am helped; my heart exults, and with my song I give thanks to him. Amen!

MY ENCOUNTER WITH ANGELS

Chapter 2
Dancing with the Angels
By Zernon S. Evans

* * * * *

I can remember the day I was baptized at a small Baptist church in my hometown. The water was cold; I didn't mind because I was proud and happy to be getting baptized. When I came up out of the water, I felt the spirit of God descend on me. I did not know specifically at that it was the Spirit of God, but I knew in my spirit it was of God.

I was twelve; I don't know what was magical about that age, when my mom sat me down one day and told me about Jesus. In that era parents made children wait until they were at least twelve before they let them get baptized. I remember how delighted I was to hear her tell of his glory and her faith in him. It was so amazing because he had been talking to me every day at school. I just didn't know his name was Jesus.

I loved him; I found my peace with him. Dad was sick and that was sad so I had to focus on something sweet and peaceful. I survived middle school and high school and, yes, my dad got better with his health issues. He lived to see all seven of his children graduate from college.

I eventually progressed to become an elementary school teacher. I loved the students, and everything about my profession but there was always something interfering and causing problems for me.

Most of the parents I worked with cooperated and were very attentive to their children and to my efforts to help their children. But it seemed like there was always one or two that found fault with me. It was so demonic. Parents that knew their children were not on grade level and knew how hard and sincerely I worked with children would find fault and complain every chance that they could.

I had a Christian co-worker who was present one day to hear a parent complain about her child's report card. The parent was saying that her child has always been on the honor roll and never made so many C's on his report card. My friend happened to be walking by and told the parent the child was in her room the year before and most certainly was not an honor roll student; then proceeded to her room and pulled a copy of his report card to show her. Needless to say, I did not have any more problems with that parent again.

The experiences with parents like that would really hurt me so bad. In retrospect I did not think of the parents who supported me I just worried about the few that didn't. The majority of my parents supported me and would thank me often. Most parents were glad that their children loved to come to school. Parents told me that their child talked about me all the time.

When I first starting teaching, all I knew was I loved my student. I didn't know how to reach them. I fussed at them, yelled at them and complained about their slow progress. One day a local minister was on campus; He walked into my room and told my students, "You all need to stop whatever you are doing that's wrong because I could hear Mrs. Evans yelling as soon as I entered the building."

That shook me up. I stared seeking God about what I should do. Once he showed me in a dream why a student was not happy at his home. One day a student was standing close to me and he sounded like he was snoring, this had happened on other occasion, also. On that day I took my hand and pushed him to the side. The voice of God said, "Don't push him away, I put him with you so that he can get help." I got up and took the student to the nurse; when she looked in his mouth, she was so upset. She called his mom to come and take him to the doctor.

They scheduled him for surgery to take his tonsils out immediately after the visit. The nurse said it was a miracle he had not died in his sleep because of the swelling and infection of his tonsils. I understood, now. My assignment was clear. I was there as an agent through which God could work with the families coming through my class.

The state that I was living in at this time gave me my biggest challenge. It was so bazaar, I was doing an excellent job with my classes but a few parents would conjure up situations to find fault. I would have migraine headaches at night and find it hard to sleep.

Sometimes through the years teachers and administrators would show resentment toward me just because they thought I was too creative. I had skits, spelling bees, speaking contest and many other events.

Teachers would make statements as, "So, you are trying to show us up." I was so hurt by their reactions. Others who really respected and admired me would come around when I was alone and compliment me. One teacher came by my room with a Christmas gift and said, "Don't tell anyone I gave you this gift."

I suffered this problems for years. I was finally working in a State where it seemed everything from hell was attacking me.

Sometimes I would spent long periods of time explaining an assignment but as soon as I released the student to do independent work they could not remember what to do. These are smart students; why can't they remember instructions? That is the question I asked God. One morning I made a point of explaining the lesson slowly and walking around to assure all students were focused. At one point, I was at the front of the room continually explaining the lesson; when I looked toward the class, I saw shadows, just like the one you see of yourself on the ground. The shadows were standing in front of the group facing me and they were holding up their hands catching my words and preventing my students from hearing my words.

I called a friend to help me figure out what was going on. My friend took me to the scripture and showed me what was happening and how to eradicate those spirits. But most importantly explained the attack and the fact that I was a threat to the enemy because he does not want my students to succeed.

I contacted other Christian teachers who were friends of mind and found that they were having similar issues. They had formed prayer groups to pray and support one another. One shared an incident where God told her to anoint her door facing of the classroom with oil. She said the next day she looked up and these little spirits were coming toward her room just walking and bouncing happily, but when they tried to step into her room there was something like a rubber band effect that popped them back on their behinds. She said she observed them get up and go into the room next door. She said over the next few months children were rebelling against the teacher, and the teacher began to get sick and miss school often.

I started praying and being aware of everything I did in the classroom. I saw immediate results in the classroom, but my supervisor started evaluating my work at a low rate, encouraging parent to call for conferences with me and logging every minute of my day, literally.

I sought God continually for guidance. After a while I notice that every time I left my room to go down the hallway I would see an angel wing, not two, just one wing, similar to the one on the book cover. It would travel before me like a shield. I did not see this image anywhere else except in the hallway at school.

I was convinced by now that I was in a battle for the students' educational and spiritual growth. But, I had peace. The migraines left and I did not react to the few parents looking for conflict.

The spirit in my supervisor was irritated. The supervisor began writing me up. Sense I would not back down, to my surprise she called for me one morning. She said something to the effect that I was insubordinate, and I was transferred to another school.

I was not worried about anything. I started humming the song I Surrender all as I gathered my belonging. I thanked God that he was my life and only he can transfer me. I started praising him for his goodness, telling him that I trusted him and thanking him for the peace I was experiencing.

I got instructions on where I was supposed to

report the next day. I was so confident that God was doing a new thing in my life. I trusted that he was in charge and I didn't have to worry about a thing.

I arrived home stilling praising him. I opened the door; I started climbing the stairs. I said in my mind Lord the word says the angels surround you and worship you. I want to come in with the angels and worship you. I was at the bathroom door.

I stepped inside the bath room into another realm I was in the mist of angels. I did not see wing like in the hallway at school, but I could hear the wing sounding like they were flapping against each other. The angles were dancing; one took my hand and turned me around. Some were very tall; some were my height. I never saw wings, but I heard them brushing together. The angels that danced with me were draped in goal, all of them were draped in gold.

They did not stop dancing with me, but I pulled back from that realm. It really was kind of frightening. I wanted God to know that I trusted him to take care of me. I wanted him to know that I was not intimidated by my experience on my job. My sincere surrender took me into a realm where I was assured that not only were angels watching over me, but I am welcome to honor and praise him in their presence.

Angels are all around you. You may not see them but know that you are covered!

Chapter 3
Angels & Worship
By Annette Birdsong

* * * * *

It all started at the age of sixteen. I had just watched a TV show about near death experiences. I had experienced one two weeks before my salvation. After seeing the show, I realized it was not my imagination and I made strange vow to God. I told

God I would surrender every area of my life to Him if He would be real to me. It was shortly after this that I was worshipping and was caught up for my first time into Paradise.

I opened my eyes to see a beautiful field with my best friend right beside me giving me the tour. It was Holy Spirit. He was invisible, but I could see His silhouette which reminded me of moving water. For the entire time I was there I could hear wonderful singing. I knew instantly it was the voice of an angel. The melody was Hebraic...filled with love, joy, peace, and it had a healing aspect. The music itself was alive and carried the life of God. Later, when Holy Spirit brought me back to myself, I was greatly surprised to hear the soprano voice flowing from my mouth. You see, until then I had never sung soprano. At that time, I was singing first tenor in my high school choir and did not know I even had a higher register. I have never forgotten that melody and for several years when I sang it I would immediately be back in Heaven again.

Supernatural things began to happen as I worshipped. I was not aware of them until people began to come to me and share what they experienced during the singing. At that time God had commanded me not to sing songs that were already written. He had me to pray a prayer each time I prepared to sing that would give Holy Spirit free reign. It was simple, but powerful. I would declare, "Holy Spirit more of You and less of me...Holy Spirit all of You and none of me." As time went on, I began to get caught up in the spirit while singing before an audience.

They were not aware of this because the singing never ended, but I knew it. There was no grid for this and no internet to search in those days. The glory realm and the supernatural were not being taught on in my part of the country; and I dared not speak of it. Only a couple of my closest friends knew. It would be years later while attending a school of the prophets that it was revealed I had worshipping angels assisting me not only in singing, but also in playing and dancing.

Through the years I have had night visions and dreams of angels teaching and imparting music to me. I would literally have open visions of worshipping in a great auditorium in heaven before a number that could not be counted. There were times I was playing the piano and felt like someone was guiding my hands. I even began to hear voices as I was playing. I have had people come to me and testify that they saw angels standing behind me, covering me with their wings, releasing light and healing, even demons screaming and fleeing as I released certain frequencies or high notes.

The most significant encounter I have had with the worshipping angels occurred during a time a crisis when I was fasting and praying for my daughter who had to have emergency surgery. I had lain prostrate in the floor of her hospital room crying out for her life and destiny.

When I finally got up and sat in the chair, I started falling asleep. It was in that place of between asleep and awake something incredible happened. Suddenly, I began to hear my spirit-man singing that song called I Need You Now. The funny thing is I sang it soulfully like a gospel singer and it was perfect...this was not my natural voice. Then a second voice joined my creating harmony. Next the angel choir joined, Holy Spirit lifted my hands and you guessed it; I was directing the choir. Since this has happened, God is now opening the ears of others to hear the angel choir when I am singing operatically.

I know this may be hard for many to believe, but God gave everything He created the ability to worship. Revelation 5:13 says, "And every created thing which is in heaven and on the earth and under the earth and on the sea, and all things in them, I heard saying, "To Him who sits on the throne, and to the Lamb, be blessing and honor and glory and dominion forever and ever." And Psalm 148:2 says, "Praise Him, all His angels; Praise Him, all His hosts!" For those who don't believe there are angel choirs will be in for a great surprise when they enter the gates of that city!

Holy Spirit told me I am not to be hide or devalue the gifts and the revelation He has placed on the inside of me any longer. There were many times Holy Spirit would tell me to release "the sound" and I would argue with Him. This stopped when He asked me one day, "Are you going to be like Saul, who sought to please the people or like David, who sought to please God?" Our worship is for God, not the people. So if any of you don't have the most pleasant voice in the congregation just remember as long as it is from your heart, God loves it!

I have to be transparent and let you know there has been great opposition in the south to prophetic worship and my operatic voice has not been appreciated by the majority in the African-American church. So Holy Spirit, the Father and Jesus came up with a great plan. They opened up a great door of opportunity to release the song of the Lord across the entire city. He blessed me with a local TV show called "In Heavenly Places". The enemy thought I was defeated because physical doors were closed, but God had a plan! You see, the way has been made now. Why has the warfare been so great? It is because prophetic worship causes Heaven and earth to collide with the glory of God!

It is an act of faith each time you open your mouth and trust God to fill it. Even the musicians must learn to flow and be led of Holy Spirit. As they move deeper into worship, they must sing songs to God rather than about Him.

Requirements for Heavenly Worship:

1. Your entire worship team must be living holy before God. Those who have clean hands and a pure heart shall ascend the mountain of God according to Psalm 24:3-4.

2. You must release control of the service to Holy Spirit. You must be willing to wait on Him. You are asking Holy Spirit to have his way and inviting all of Heaven to worship with you.

3. You must know the prophetic words you release in song will activate the angels because you are singing and declaring the Father's precise will for that moment... giving the people their DAILY bread; not yesterday's. You are to hear and release the word of the Lord for today and tomorrows victories. Yesterday is done and gone.

4. You must declare to God that you receive the ministry of the angels and gifts they have brought according to Hebrews 1:14.

5. You must teach your congregation how

to enter the glory realm by giving true worship to God with great expectation and obeying instructions given during the worship. It may be dancing, shouting, giving an offering, etc. The Father is looking for those who worship Him in spirit and truth according to John 4:23-24.

6. Once your church has become adjusted to entering deeper worship, allow them time to release their song to the Lord by singing in the spirit (tongues). This will open up another dimension of glory according to Ephesians 5:18-19.

7. You must allow the people time to get still before God and wait. Allow Holy Spirit to finish what He has begun. In other words, wait until the anointing lifts. You don't rush out of the presence of the King of Kings. This is the time when many will see visions, encounter angels and the Lord, receive a prophetic word and miracles come forth that are yet to be revealed.

Of course, this does not happen overnight. The

people must be taught on the importance of worship. Depending on where you church is in the scope of things, it may take quite some time to transform them into a body of prophetic worshippers. You as the leader must stir up a hunger in them for more of God. They must desire to see Heaven come to earth. With your determination and grace of the Holy Spirit, it can be done.

Remember, God is enthroned on the praises of His people. Angels are drawn to wherever there is true worship being released. They bring gifts, mantles, answers to prayer, healing, provision…and they war for us due to our praise according to II Chronicles 20:20-25:

Judah and you inhabitants of Jerusalem: Believe in the Lord your God, and you shall be established; believe His prophets, and you shall prosper."

21 And when he had consulted with the people, he appointed those who should sing to the Lord, and who should praise the beauty of holiness, as they went out before the army and were saying:

"Praise the Lord, For His mercy endures forever."

22 Now when they began to sing and to praise, the Lord set ambushes against the people of Ammon, Moab, and Mount Seir, who had come against Judah; and they were defeated. 23 For the people of Ammon and Moab stood up against the inhabitants of Mount Seir to utterly kill and destroy them. And when they had made an end of the inhabitants of Seir, they helped to destroy one another.

24 So when Judah came to a place overlooking the wilderness, they looked toward the multitude; and there were their dead bodies, fallen on the earth. No one had escaped.

25 When Jehoshaphat and his people came to take away their spoil, they found among them an abundance of valuables on the dead bodies, and precious jewelry, which they stripped off for themselves, more than they could carry away; and they were three days gathering the spoil because there was so much. (NKJV)

This story is an example of what happens in the earth when we as children of God release our praise in obedience to the prophetic word of the Lord. They were vindicated in the eyes of all, they did not have to fight the battle and they received supernatural provision for all they needed. Praising God in times of distress is an act of faith. It causes all of Heaven to move on your behalf. Never allow the devil to steal your praise.

MY ENCOUNTER WITH ANGELS

Chapter 4
Lifted and Delivered
By Lolitia Newman
* * * * *

We were in Memphis, Tennessee. My mother had taken my sister and I to our aunt's house. I cannot recall why we were there, but we had several family members there: aunts and cousins. Our parents sent us out to play in the back of the apartment complex. We played as family does; kids just having a great time.

I had to have been about 5 years old or so because I remember not having started grammar school yet. While we were playing around the pool, one of the kids pushed me into the swimming pool. I remember going down, fighting under the water to get to the top; fighting - because I had never been in a pool before nor did I know how to swim.

All of the kids left, and no one tried to help me. I just remember going down and fighting, and the more I fought, the more I sank... until I blacked out. Somehow, I came to and became conscious, and I felt hands as though the palms supported my body like a board (what I now know to have been an angel, was massive and its hands covered my whole body), began thrusting me up towards the surface of the pool – like I was jet propelled. I opened my eyes and saw a florescent, yellowish-green like color. The wings were moving in a waving motion in the water. The faster the wings moved, the quicker we went to the top. I could see the sun light becoming brighter as we went higher. I had never seen something so beautiful and bright. I could not see its face; it was behind me.

When we got to the top, it stood me upright, pressing the water out of me while it remained in the water. I began coughing, water came out of my nose and my lungs. Then the angel turned me around and pointed to my aunt's house. I walked in the direction that the angel pointed until I reached my aunt's patio door. I called for my mother. When she saw me, she screamed and said, "Oh, my God! What happened to you?" I was drenched from head to toe. I pointed to the other child who had pushed me into the pool and told my mother what occurred. I told her, "an angel got me out of the pool". She began to weep and express her feelings of sadness and discontent as none of the children told her or any adult what happened to me at the pool.

One Touch

I was about eight or nine years old, a tomboy, playing in the peach tree field. It was nighttime and I was out catching fireflies. I was running and I did not see the brick. I hit my foot on the brick. This changed my life forever, it set me on a journey called faith that would allow me to have an encounter with the healing angel – the great physician, God himself touched me.

The sun was going down; it was dusk. I was running through the field because it was an abundance of fireflies that night on the side of my uncle's house—running through his peach, apple, plum trees. I would climb up the trees and send some down to my cousins. We would give them to my aunt so that she could make pies for us.

I did not see the brick that I ran into. I fell and held my foot, and I barely made it home. Over the next couple of days, I made it back outside to discover that I hit my foot on a stone. I told my mother and she took me to the doctors. From that point, I went on many doctor's appointments. I went through a series of medicinal/steroid shots in my foot and nothing relieved the pain. They stuck needles the length of my pointy finger in and out of my joints. It was horrible, excruciating pain, and nothing was helping. My foot became stiff to the point I could not move it backwards and forwards. I remember waking up having to crawl to the bathroom. I was in constant agonizing pain.

Due to the excruciating pain and the fact that it would lock up on me, it prevented me from doing youthful activities. I began to gain weight. I recall one day crying so bad because I was in so much pain. I told my mother, "Mama my foot hurts so bad. I want God to heal my foot." She said, "Well, if you ask God and believe, he will heal your foot. He will." She also told me to, "ask God to send the healing angel."

We took a trip to Champaign, IL. to visit Sheriff Temple A.O.H. Church. I sat on the second pew on the left side of the church near the middle aisle. The then, Overseer Wright opened the bible. He said that we would do offering differently. He opened it to the scripture,

Matthew 7:7-8 (KJV) Ask, and it shall be given you; seek, and ye shall find; knock, and it shall be opened unto you: For every one that asketh receiveth; and he that seeketh findeth; and to him that knocketh it shall be opened."

He said bring your offering and put your offering in the bible and ask God what you want and believe what you ask for. The entire church lined up for the processional while the organist played music. I stood in line and all I could think about was what my mother needed, "My momma needs money, she needs…" as I limped all the way to the offering table.

All I continued to think about was what she needed. I could see my mother speaking in tongues because the elders and minsters came first. Other people who had gone before me were rejoicing in the Lord and speaking in tongues.

When I came to the table, and I put my offering on the bible. All I could hear, screaming out of my soul, was "my feet, my feet." I took my hand off and jumped back. I looked around to see if anyone else could hear me. I went to put my hand back on the bible and I heard it again, "my feet, my feet."

Romans 8:26 "Likewise the Spirit also helpeth our infirmities: for we know not what we should pray for as we ought: but the Spirit itself maketh intercession for us with groanings which cannot be uttered."

Even though I was interceding for my mother, God was interceding for me about my feet.

After I lifted my hands from the bible, I limped all the way to the second pew crying because I heard God interceding for me about my feet when I placed my hand on the bible. I knew the whole church had heard it.

When I got back to my seat... crying profusely, all I could say was "thank you Jesus, thank you Jesus." At that point I realized the healing angel numbed my feet; I began to put weight on my other foot for support. Then something strange happened, I saw my foot lift off the floor, I began to hear bones crack and I saw my foot twist, but I did not feel it. It would twist and crack and twist. I began to yell in the church, "MAMA HE'S HEALING MY FEET RIGHT NOW!" My mother ran over and saw God healing my feet and she began to shout down the middle aisle. Bishop Wright began to shout.

He numbed me from my knees down. I did not feel anything, but I watched him do it. He took my other foot and began to do the same for it.

From that day forward, I never saw another physician. I never got another shot. That day, God answered my prayer that my mother told me to ask for. I have been able to live a normal life. I still have a curve in my foot to remind me. I have never had to crawl again. He told me that I had healing virtue for other people.

MY ENCOUNTER WITH ANGELS

Chapter 5
Invoking Angelic Release

By Jennifer Washington

* * * * *

I've been able to see into the spiritual realm for as long as I can remember. When I was in my earlier teens, I specifically began to get activated in my spiritual gifts. I used to attend a school of the prophets with my mother and little sister. I believe that stirred a lot up in me. Both the gifts that may have been dormant and becoming stronger in the areas that had already come to the forefront as well. My mother was a seer as well so these things became very familiar to me.

As a young girl, I always loved music. It's no surprise that a lot of angelic encounters began to happen as worship was going forth. I noticed that releasing different words and sounds would cause angelic forces to be activated and released to complete their assignment on the earth. That assignment could have been to help or heal an individual, or even a group of people or a church. Whatever God sent them to do could be done when we activated them with our words or song.

Why is that so? Psalm 103:20 says Bless the Lord, ye his angels, that excel in strength, that do his commandments, hearkening unto the voice of his word. Releasing the word through song is like a hallmark for me, especially in certain scenarios. I will give a couple of examples here soon. The angels respond so quickly to this type of release. I've been in places where the angels were literally just waiting there, standing and looking. It was like they were searching for the person or people in the room that would finally release the word, release the command so that they could go complete their assignment.

How many times do we as a congregation enter into a "house of worship" and remain insensitive to the angelic assistants that the Lord has given us? Even as I write, the Holy Spirit is reiterating that Jesus is not only the Lord of Hosts, but he is the Kings of kings, the Lord of Lords.

What does that mean for us? We know He is the God of the angel armies. We sometimes forget that those kings and lords he speaks of are Christians. We are made in the image of God. The blood of Christ Jesus runs through our veins. This is where we can be assured in our authority in the earth. We re-present Christ in the earth. So in relation to this subject of angels, Christ commands the angel armies. We are like Christ, so we can command the angels as well.

These angels are not only messengers, but they also serve. Who do they serve? The heirs of salvation. Hebrews 1:14 says, are they not all ministering spirits, sent forth to minister for them who shall be heirs of salvation? (KJV)

The NASB version says, are they not all ministering spirits, sent out to render service for the sake of those who will inherit salvation?

The NLT version says, therefore, angels are only servants – spirits sent to care for people who will inherit salvation.

If you notice, it says will inherit salvation. If you consider that, you can easily understand when people say, guardian or protective angels. Most of the time, these are the angels you are given as soon as you enter the world. I would even say while you were in the womb of your mother they were there. Why? Because you were technically already in the earth realm.

They are sent to serve, care for, minister to, protect you and more! I said all that to encourage you to know that angels are real and they are listening for your commands through the voice of the word. Now let me give a couple of examples.

One of my gifts is found in the art of poetry. I started writing when I was a kid. I used to win different contests for the execution of that gift. I loved writing. As I got older, I suffered even more abuse and I stopped writing altogether. In 2012, I rededicated my life back to the Lord. It was around that time that I prayed that all my gifts would be restored and even magnified. It was then that the Lord began to give me prophetic poetry. A lot of times it would include the written word of God at some point. These were some powerful poems. There were times I would even weep as the Lord would pour these words onto the pages.

As I have progressed over the years, I now notice angelic release as I am ministering. Some times people will weep as an angel is standing near them releasing healing to them or their inner man. Sometimes they touch the person, sometimes they don't. They also release more than healing. It just depends on what the person or group is in need of. We must always remember that God is a good father, He is always wanting to meet our needs. Sometimes, the angels are there to help meet that need.

There are many times that I have been rebuked to even taking on the cares and pressures of life. I got rebuked because I wasn't using my angelic help. I was trying to accomplish things in my own strength.

I remember needing some money to fund a new business that was in my heart to start. I went to pray an agreement and declaration prayer about it with my mom. In that declaration, we stated that we looked down into the earth from our seated positions in heaven, and commanded the finances to be released. We commanded my financial angels to go out and bring the funds back to me according to the word. I literally was given the money within two days, from an unlikely source. What if I didn't release my angels to go out and bring me what I needed? Would I still have gotten the money? There was no striving in this approach. Sometimes, God wants to make things easy for us, but we choose the hard way. We choose the "if I can work these hours of overtime, I'll have enough way." We have to move beyond that. God has angelic help for each of us!

He truly cares, there have been several moments when I was driving in my car, and a friend would say, I see you have four angels protecting you and your car right now. There are two on each side. What is that? God cares. And He sent His ministering spirits to care for us.

Once again I'll admit, most of my encounters have come while ministering in song. I'm a psalmist. That's how I flow, especially in the prophetic. There are times where people will be getting ordained or commissioned to do something and I just can't give a "normal word." I am compelled to release the song of the Lord over that person. Sometimes I can hear the angels singing with me, which is pretty normal. But other times, it feels like the angel's voice I coming out of my voice while I sing. There is a weight that comes over me and sometimes I'm just weeping as I sing. But there is a power coming through my voice even as weep. Some of my ministry companions call me a "weeping prophet." I'd say that is pretty accurate. God is compassionate and He cares. I believe that's His compassion that comes out as those notes are released.

An angel of Joy was assigned to me a while ago. A lot of times, the Lord will have me release my angel of joy to minister to His people. Supernatural joy comes a rids them of these scattered places of sorrow that they have been chained too. It's an amazing thing to watch.

I also see angels that release peace.

One thing that tends to be consistent is seeing angel armies during worship. Especially a song of the Lord type of flow. These tend to be songs of declaration and more often than not, songs of righteous judgment that the God of Might is releasing. Sometimes things are going on in the land that needs to be rectified. Unholy and unrighteous laws, statutes and judgments in a city, region, state or country are things the God takes to heart and those things have to be righteously judged. In these moments we command them to go do what God is speaking.

I have also seen God appoint an angelic guard around and behind those who operate or will as generals in the spirit.

I have seen angels fully dressed in armor bowed down in worship. How powerful is that?! I couldn't do anything but bow down and continue to worship with them.

Did you know that joining in with the angels and singing holy, holy, holy will cause them to come and worship with you? Why? Because you are joining in with their eternal song. It never ends. If you join in, that puts you in one accord with heaven, just like that!

Our Father is truly amazing. He has given us angels as servants and weapons so we are not "in this thang alone." Be encouraged. Ask the Father to open your eyes to to see the angels assigned to you. If you seek, you will find. God does not desire for us to be in the dark. He desires to reveal his mysteries. All you have to do it ask.

MY ENCOUNTER WITH ANGELS

Chapter 6

The Delta

By Antonico Thomas

* * * * *

My first memory of an encounter that I can vividly remember was on my first ministry prayer in the Delta. We were praying about strategy for this prayer mission. We began to pray and sing. The worship was very high. As we drove my first vision was a dark shadow flee fast past the car in the opposite direction. Next, I saw a huge foot larger than the car with a leather sandal on laced up. As my eyes with up to see what it was a feeling of fear came over me. And then I knew the fear of the Lord came upon me. I did not want to move. The angel had on a white and gold robe. The gold was so bright like I've never seen before. The angel had a bow and arrows that never ended. The angel began to shoot the arrows in different directions then another angel appeared and began to shoot in different directions also. Then a third joined and began to swing its wings. As in Proverbs 14:26 In the fear of the lord is strong confidence; and his children shall have a place of refuge.

The feeling that came over me was so strong that tears began to roll down my face I had no words to speak. I was scared and bewildered and could not believe what I was seeing. I looked at everyone in the car and no one acted as if they saw what I saw. As we prayed more in our heavenly language they warred with the commands from our prayers. This feeling was overwhelming to believe or even see in person. As we kept driving a hand lifted the car and carried us into where we were going. After I got home one of the ladies called me and asked, "what did you see?" I was silent. She said Holy spirit told her I saw something.

So, I told her what I saw, and she told me that it's ok if I see things others don't see. She continued to say that people may not see what I see, and that I'm not crazy. A sense of relief came over me that someone believed me. At first when I would tell people things I saw. I would get strange looks like it was not true. But God kept showing me things others did not see. I felt like I could not tell everyone. Because nobody else would see the things God allowed me to see.

My next encounter was at a conference. And as soon as I walked in and sat down an angel was there actually waving at me. I thought to myself this is different. I sat down and the service began. The worship began and the angel was flying, and another joined in and the wings began to move. Next the speaker came up and the angel began to go back and forth to the heavens. As in 1 Peter 1:12 unto whom it is revealed, that not unto themselves, but unto us they did minister the things; which are now reported unto you by them that have preached the gospel unto you with the Holy Ghost sent down from the heavens; which things the angels desire to investigate. This means to me the angels report to God about the worship and the word being released over the people. These angels were worshipping and praising God.

My next encounter was not seen but felt. One Saturday morning I was in my bed and my son came in. And I was reading, and I told him lets pray. We began to pray and praise. We also began to sing. I had been praying for weeks for my heavenly language.

As we prayed my son yelled out mommy angels are coming in the room, I felt the power of the holy Spirit. He then said mommy hold your hand out I asked why he said they have presents for you. So, I held my hands out and he said let me open it he said it was keys I thanked God for them not knowing what they were for. We started back praying and words came out I did not know and then my son said with excitement Holy spirt said that is what you prayed for.

He could have never known this only God knew what I prayed for. I began to weep with joy. As in Matthew 16:27 For the son of man is going to come in his father's glory with his angels, and then h will reward each person according to what they have done. My faith and praise broke open the heavens for God to release a gift to pray in my heavenly language with new words. I was so grateful for God releasing the gift of tongues.

My next encounter was when my son had a bad experience with torment of bad dreams. I prayed for a few days and one night I saw in my hall way a angel with Gold armor head to toe with one opening with a shield and sword. I was frozen with the fear of the Lord again. I saw the word protection. So next I got out my bed and walked up to the angel and looked I saw no eyes no face. Later, I would find out this angel protects my son. And his purpose and wars for him with only the commands from the words of the lord. the more God gave me wisdom and knowledge the scriptures command the angels. So the movement became different with only scripture and praying in the spirit.

My son could pray in the spirt and it would move faster. Later I would only see this specific angel with certain people with authority. As time went by, I began to ask what the different angels do and what they mean. God began to give me types and who they are and what they do. It's many for different purposes. What they bring their function and what God uses them for. One thing we all need to understand is we do not worship angels nor should we talk to them like asking questions or put our faith in them they are heavenly host God gives us to command with his word to war and bring things to us and to fight in the spirt along with prayer to move in the heavens. They are not our friends and they worship God so never talk to them.

Some bring wisdom, some bring to edify the body. Some fight on your behalf some come with authority and mantels and some come in times of trouble. Some have finances and I could go on and on but it so many I cannot put it all here. To God be the glory and I thank God for revelation and wisdom to trust me with these downloads and vision for my purpose in my life. And I want to say how grateful for the blood of Jesus that covers us all without him I am nothing. Thank you, Jesus, for laying your life down for me.

Dr. Juanita Woodson

Dr. Juanita Woodson is an author, counselor, coach, speaker, and entrepreneur. She is the CEO of Impact Ministries Global, Impact Book Publishing Company, and Impact Development Foundation. Dr. Woodson is an apostolic and a prophetic voice with a healing and deliverance ministry who believes in the power of prophecy and prayer. She travels the world alongside her husband on ministry mission and business trips to several countries. Testimonies of breakthrough and deliverance are shared by many both nationally and internationally.

Dr. Woodson has pioneered and founded several non-profit family advocacy organizations that have acquired over $1.5 million in renewable grants. Education, training, counseling and advocacy are all components of her non-profit belief system. She is a mompreneur who built several businesses from home. She has founded Impact Books, a publishing company that provides self-publishers with all the tools and support services they need. She is an author, coach, family advocate and inspirational speaker.

Dr. Woodson has written sever books including "Date For Deliverance", "Women's Deliverance Devotional", "Anointed But Sick" (soon to be a short film), "Beauty In The Pulpit" which was featured on Atlanta Live 57 WATC TV, "Encounter With Angels", she has co-authored "Your Child My Student" with Dr .Shekina Farr Moore, (as seen in Forbes Magazine, Black Enterprise and Huffington Post). She has been a repeat writer for The Elijah's List. She has also taught dream interpretation for a summit on the "I Need A Word" network platform.

Dr. Woodson has a Doctorate and Master's degree in Christian Counseling from Jacksonville Theological Seminary. Her Bachelor's degree studies are in Psychology and History from Eastern Illinois University, Virginia Commonwealth University and the University of the West Indies in Cave Hill, Barbados.

Her mandate is to equip individuals to become everything that God promised they could be and have everything God promised they could have! She is available for personal coaching and counseling sessions.

Dr. Juanita Woodson
950 Eagles Landing Pkwy
Suite 722
Stockbridge, GA 30281
(678) 614-0016

www.drjuanitawoodson.com
www.impactbookco.com

www.ingramcontent.com/pod-product-compliance
Lightning Source LLC
Chambersburg PA
CBHW052101070526
44584CB00017B/2281